DIFFERENTIATED INSTRUCTION IN THE TEACHING PROFESSION

Innovative ways to change how we teach

Kristen Koppers

EduMatch Publishing

Differentiated Instruction in the
Teaching Profession
Kristen Koppers

Published by EduMatch®
PO Box 150324, Alexandria, VA 22315
www.edumatchpublishing.com

These books are available at special discounts
when purchased in quantities of 10 or more for
use as premiums, promotions fundraising, and
educational use. For inquiries and details, contact
the publisher: sarah@edumatch.org.

ISBN-13: 978-1-970133-16-5

"In *Differentiated Instruction in the Teaching Profession,* Kristen not only takes us on her journey, and the journeys of others, to inspire us to be better. She also incorporates research, references, and hard data to support the ideas and mind-shifts throughout." — Jeff Gargas, COO/Co-founder, Teach Better Team

"*DI in the Teaching Profession* gets to the heart of three things we should hold sacred when it comes to learning institutions...relationships, authenticity, and connection. Kristen has done a great job of highlighting how to make them happen in any school, in any place, at any level." — Joe Sanfelippo, Superintendent, Fall Creek School District

"Great ideas for student learning and differentiation."
— Beata Blaho, Teacher, University of Chicago Lab School

"The book is soundly written. Kristen did an excellent job detailing her thoughts and experiences in the classroom. The Educator Connection additions were awesome. It's good to see other voices integrated with the author's."
— Dr. William Deyamport, III, Instructional Technologist, Hattiesburg School District

Contents

Dedication

First, I would like to say "Thank you" to all in my PLN for the help during the four-year process of writing this book. Without your insight, I am not sure if I would have completed the project. Second, I want to thank Maggie Maslowski, my educator-in-crime, for her continuous belief that we can make a difference no matter how many obstacles we face, personally and professionally. Last, this book would not have been created if it weren't for attending the *What Great Educators Do Differently* conference held in 2015. Thanks to Jeff Zoul, Jimmy Casas, Todd Whitaker, and most of all, Joe Sanfelippo. This is where I began to write my story.

Ch. 1: Where it All Began

My Story

Before I was teaching, I earned a Bachelor of Arts degree in English/Journalism and minored in Practical Writing. I wanted to be a journalist and focus my career on print media. I soon found out that a career as a journalist, as a full-time job, wasn't what I thought it was, even though I've been writing since the age of 12. Newly married and with my mom being ill, I needed to have dependable income. I learned that I was able to apply for a substitute teaching certificate with my Bachelor of Arts degree. I didn't know it then, but I soon discovered my passion. I went through the process to become a certified substitute teacher.

After substituting for a little over a year, I discovered that I wanted a class of my own. Three years later, earning a small income with part-time jobs and with my mom getting better, I went back to school to earn a Master's in English with a secondary education certificate, which enabled me to seek a full-time position as a secondary education teacher.

As a first-year teacher, I was excited to start my career. I wanted to make a difference and follow in the footsteps of my sophomore--year high school

Geology teacher, Mr. Niznik. I remember how he made class interesting by bringing students into the conversation or focusing on helping them succeed. I originally took the class to meet one of the science requirements. At that age, I was not about to dissect a frog. Instead of focusing on assessments and grades, Mr. Niznik ensured that I understood the material. His reason for teaching was not to satisfy the requirements but rather to help his students learn. He not only made the class fun, but also interesting by adding humor, forging connections, and most of all, by using different learning strategies. He was one of the few teachers who "taught outside of the box." He not only *taught* his students, but he was also able to motivate them in class and school.

***

What I learned in my first year of teaching was not something that can be learned from a book. No one can teach a new teacher the nuances of discipline in the classroom, how to communicate with parents, and, of course, how to approach the long hours of planning lessons and grading at home. Throughout this book, I offer strategies on how to change the way we teach instead of modifying assignments. Some amazing educators agreed to share their stories of successes. They shared their passion for using differentiated instruction strategies. Each can impact students not just through words but also through actions.

Change the Way Students Learn

As a high school English teacher, I taught dozens of novels by deconstructing them to create a novel study. Kurt Vonnegut's, *Slaughterhouse Five* (1969), ended up being the most popular novels with my seniors. Given scheduling in my district, it was possible to teach the same group of students over multiple years. In fact, I often had my previous sophomores as seniors. We flashbacked to what was taught sophomore year to deconstructing novels senior year. While reading *Slaughterhouse Five,* we discussed the possible existence of the Fourth Dimension, including the philosophical aspects of free will, time travel, and character attributes based on the author's life. We studied the characters' reasons for their actions during the course of the novel to enhance students' cognitive learning.

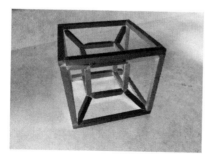

The cube is significant to the novel, Slaughterhouse Five, as it represents the Fourth Dimension through portals. As you look through the cube, you can see all the sides. However, in reality, we are unable to "see through" the cube and can only view what's in front of us, to the side of us, and above us.

Throughout reading the novel, students began to think about whether time actually existed due to the "portals" that the main character was able to travel through.

Focus on Teaching Students instead of Standards

> It's not about changing the curriculum or going against the standards; it's about focusing on a different perspective.

While many educators literally follow the curriculum from point-to-point, there are times that teachers need to focus on using differentiated instruction.

It's not about changing the curriculum or going against the standards; it's about focusing on a different perspective.

I realized that I needed to focus on each student as an individual. While some may understand how to read Vonnegut's *Slaughterhouse Five* without clarification, others find it challenging to read as it does not follow a natural chronological progression of events. Students that show difficulty with reading may need extra help understanding the context of the story. There are a variety of ways to help students understand what they are reading.

One of the simplest ways to use differentiated instruction is to use context clues to comprehend unfamiliar words. Sometimes, understanding certain words and definitions refocuses the student. Context clues also increase students' understanding as they work in small groups. Even reading in pairs will help students have a better understanding of the words and content. In their groups, they can share their ideas. Learning from a classmate increases the understanding of a topic that may be new to them. For the students who are challenged by reading *Slaughterhouse Five*, small group discussion gave them the opportunity for a better understanding. Just like *Slaughterhouse Five*, many students find it difficult to understand the complexities of Charlotte Perkins Gilman's *The Yellow Wallpaper* (1892).

Students often have difficulty understanding Perkins' main character, the narrator, as they see her as a woman who becomes a schizophrenic by being locked up in a room. However, there is more to the story than a mother who suffers from postpartum depression. She is a woman who has an internal conflict, struggling with her own identity. Instead of teaching the short story the traditional way following the plot structure and pursuing character analysis, I help students to understand the woman's point of view of how being kept captive created her sense of imprisonment. They use critical thinking skills to understand not only the character, but also to develop empathy for others facing comparable situations in contemporary times.

Assessing Students' Knowledge

In order to use differentiated instruction in the classroom, teachers need to assess their students' understanding. According to Tomlinson, Moon, and Imbeau, authors of *Assessment and Student Success in a Differentiated Classroom* (2013), pre-assessments are "meant to give the teacher a sense of the range of needs in the class that are relative to the unit's standards" (p. 5). Such assessments determine what students already know and what they need to know after completing a unit.

Pre-assessments help teachers plan lessons. Teachers can create activities to ensure that all students are learning the material based on their own abilities. When designing a pre-assessment for a specific unit of study, teachers should focus on what they want their students to learn during the unit. "It's helpful to consider pre-assessments separately because their goals and uses are slightly different from those of formative or ongoing assessments, which occur throughout a unit" (Tomlinson et al., 2013, p. 5). Pre-assessments help with grouping students of differing abilities, so stronger students can assist struggling students.

Ch. 2: Encouragement, Not Discouragement

Creating Differentiated Instruction in the Classroom

As teachers, we can motivate our students by focusing on Differentiated Instruction (DI) strategies. Such strategies create a way for teachers to focus on each student's individualized learning needs. Tomlinson et al. (as cited in Wesley, 2014) notes: "Differentiated Instruction is factoring students' individual learning styles and levels of readiness first *before* designing a lesson plan. Research on the effectiveness of differentiation shows this method benefits a wide range of students, from those with learning disabilities to those who are considered high ability." DI learning encourages students; we need to know their strengths and weaknesses and what they already know. Many students feel discouraged when they cannot complete an assignment or get help while at home, which can lead to "shutting" down or giving up.

I wanted to differentiate the way work is completed in class, because I saw how it hindered my students from wanting to learn. Homework can create a sense of unwanted anxiety, stress, and sleep deprivation. For two years, I changed "homework" to work that could be done in class to ensure understanding of the material. In *Ditch that Homework,* Matt Miller and Alice Keeler (2017) suggest that using DI does not mean changing a worksheet or requiring additional practice for a student. DI is about the learning process. Miller and Keeler stress that additional practice does not necessarily help a student. "Rigor does not equate to quantity. Giving students more work to do at home does not increase the rigor of the course" (Miller & Keeler, 2017, p. 98).

> Homework can create a sense of unwanted anxiety, stress, and sleep deprivation.

Likewise, giving more practice work in class does not necessarily deepen understanding of a concept, and some students might shut down instead of focusing on what they need to learn. With this in mind, I was determined to help all students. As a high school teacher, I know that it is extremely difficult to get around the room in a 55-minute period helping 30 students. So, what happens to the students who do not get the help they need? They might end up confused. After I understood the learning needs of my students, I placed them in groups with peers of different learning abilities. This method enabled students that knew the material to help their peers while I walked around the room to assist as needed. In addition, this approach created a camaraderie, building relationships and contributing to motivation.

Using Differentiated Instruction

In the high school that I teach, the students and I invest in each other every day. For 180 days, students enter a classroom for approximately 55-minutes in one period, equaling to 9,900 minutes — 165 hours a year. Because students spend most of their time in school, teachers have a chance to encourage students every day. Every year, I calculate the approximate number of students that I have taught. While I cannot say I have been successful with all of them, I can say with pride that I tried to connect with every one of my students to the best of my ability.

***

In one scenario, before the students entered the room, I wrote down on the whiteboard how to write an essay. As I looked over the instructions with examples, they seemed clear to me. As the bell rang, students entered the room, chatting with their friends, checking text messages, and posting to social media. But as the tardy bell rang, I immediately got their attention by asking them to take out a pen and paper for notes. Within minutes, students looked at the board, and I could see the fear in their eyes. I made the one crucial mistake that teachers have been making for years. All the notes were already on the board before students entered the room.

Then came the question educators fear: "Miss, do we have to write all this down?" My first reaction was to say, "yes, of course, you do." But then as I looked at the board from a student's perspective, I realized that my "easy-to-read" notes were similar to asking students to create a new computer program using binary code. So, I turned to the student and simply said, "no." I erased what I wrote on the board and showed them that taking notes doesn't have to be a chore.

Methods of Notetaking

Note-taking is a skill that many of us learned in school. Students still copy down the notes word-for-word, take them home, sometimes look at them, and then shove them back in their book bag. I didn't realize that I had a hand in this meaningless process. Many times, teachers write information on the board for students to write down in their notes without realizing that it could be overload. Even using DI in notetaking, students still may fear not having enough time to take notes or not copying enough information. While some information is useful and helpful for students, I let them choose how they want to take notes. For years, I had students use a mind map to create their notes. Because many of my students "doodle" in class, mind mapping or "clustering" is another way for them to take notes.

Attending the University School of Milwaukee, Summer Spark Conference, I learned about sketch noting from Carrie Baughcum, a special education teacher in Arlington Heights, Illinois. She introduced the idea that note-taking does not have to be tedious. Sketch noting is another note-taking method with visuals added to the notes.

When I first introduced sketch noting to my students, they didn't know if I was joking or serious. As I drew (not very well) on the board, I explained how the mind continues to process the information through writing

words or creating images. I continued to talk, and students continued to listen as they drew. Students began to be creative in their lettering by adding polka dots to bubble letters or drawing a hospital instead of writing the word. Their attention focused on me and the notes; because their mind was focused while taking notes, they were also able to retain the information as they crafted their notes.

In addition to sketch noting, there are other strategies available to students. Following Cornell University's 6-2-2 method, (*Cornell University,* n.d.), a paper is divided into three sections. The first two sections are separated at the top of the paper. The note-taking column is where students write down notes during class, readings, or on their own. The cue-column is for students to write down questions after class to help clarify meanings or questions for the teacher to address the next day in case any of the notes seemed unclear.

The Cornell Note-Taking system, n.d. Retrieved from Cornell University

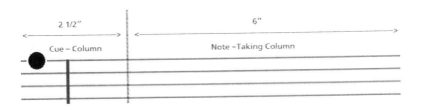

Towards the bottom of the paper, students create a horizontal line for a summary of the day's notes.

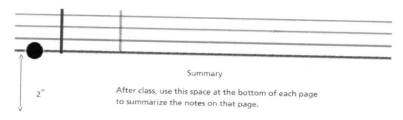

Summary

After class, use this space at the bottom of each page
to summarize the notes on that page.

2″

This method can be adapted to fit the needs of the student. Using the Cornell note-taking system, I modified this method by dividing the paper in half where students take notes on their own in one column. During class, students will add any notes from small or large group discussions. In the summary section at the bottom of the paper, students still write what they learned in class that day as a reflection piece.

Students' notes are meant for their understanding of how they will remember ideas relevant to instruction. They can choose a note-taking ability that is best for them to understand the material. Miller and Keeler (2017) offer additional ways for students to take notes in class in their book. "When taking notes, synthesize instead of copying. Recording information improves retention, but copying information is a low-cognitive skill, as it does little to nothing to help the brain remember what has been taught" (Miller & Keeler, 2017, pp. 89-90).

This method can be adapted to fit the needs of the student. I modified the Cornell note-taking system having students divide the paper in half. They took notes on their own in one column and added notes from small or large group discussions

> If we allow students with various skill levels to get help from their peers in sports and other activities, then why can't we do likewise in the classroom?

in the second column. In the summary section at the bottom of the paper, students wrote what they learned in class that day.

Compassion, not Indifference

Every year I find a few students who need extra encouragement, whether they lack it at home or at school. Their self-confidence is low, sometimes evident in their behavior or lack of progress. In addition, some students do not normally ask for help because they do not feel a student-teacher connection.

Take sports, for instance — not all players come with the same skills. By this, I mean that not all players are at the same level of competition. Some may have to practice more, while others need help from their peers. Just like teachers, coaches are not able to help all students during one practice. If we allow students with various skill levels to get help from their peers in sports and other activities, then why can't we do likewise in the classroom? It's simple: we can. Being compassionate towards our students does not make us weak or (as I thought in the past) an "easy target." It shows that we are there to help them succeed, not to watch them fail.

While I thought that I lost so many students, I found that I didn't. Recently, I met up with a student I taught over 10 years ago as a sophomore. As teachers, sometimes we get that "don't look or talk to me in public" face when we see students outside of school. Surprisingly, he came up to me and thanked me for the encouragement I gave him when he was in my class.

I remember how one of my past students would sit in the back, focusing on our class discussions. I attended graduation the year he left the high school, wondering if I made an impact on my students. Ten years later, at our school's girls' soccer game, he came up to me to say hi. He hadn't changed a bit. He told me that he was the girls' assistant soccer coach and where he was teaching. I was proud that he went into teaching because he had that type of determination in high school. But he said that he became an English teacher because of me. At that moment, I knew that I did something right.

Recently, with the help of social media, more students have contacted me to let me how what they were doing since they graduated. While we think that we do not have a lasting impression on our old students, we do. We connect with our students on different levels. Students want to feel appreciated and understood. Teaching is a stressful job, but we recharge ourselves and start a new day. Just like coaches making long-lasting impressions with their players, teachers do the same every day with their students.

Making Reading Adjustments

I realized that students don't *hate* being at school. They just are not challenged enough to pique their interest. Implementing differentiated instruction in the classroom often begins as gradual shifts. Teaching Shakespeare in a short amount of time can be difficult as Old English is hard to understand. While reading *Twelfth Night* (1602) in class, students took an interest in the play. Normally, I would have the audio to play for students to follow along as they took notes. However, one time, I decided to have students read the play as a large group activity. When students came across a word that they were unsure of or could not pronounce, other students helped with the pronunciation and understanding. By reading the play aloud, students were attentive and actively reading along.

While this may not be an individualized type of instruction, I provided students with a choice of how they wanted to read the play. Before reading *Twelfth Night*, students were asked if they wanted to read the play aloud, listen to the audio, or read silently. In the past, those who wanted to read silently were grouped in one part of the classroom so that they could read at their own pace while those who wanted to listen to the audio could do so with their headphones. This time, students as a class choose how they wanted to read the play. By giving them that choice, they assumed ownership in their learning.

Literature Circles, as a formative assessment, helped students retain the information as they read. Students were to complete certain sections of the assignment as the roles among students changed each week. Students were able to learn leadership skills as well as retain information from the reading. For more information on Literature Circles or examples used in my classroom.

DI Website:
www.kristenkoppers.wixsite.com/diteaching

Questions for Further Reflection:

1. The dynamics of homework have changed, just as the role of being an educator has. From the traditional classroom to online learning, homework has taken on a different role. In what way is homework viewed in your class?

2. How can homework be more student-driven?

3. When teachers think of using Differentiated Instruction, there is sometimes a negative connotation that every assignment needs to be modified. How can Differentiated Instruction help all students?

Ch. 3: Logical vs. "Correct" Answers

Logical answers are viewed in several ways. One is for the answer to be right or wrong based on the information provided. Another is that there is no "correct" answer, but rather an understanding that multiple possible responses could be correct. We check to make sure that students know *how* they got to their answer.

In math, objective reasoning is used when formulas are given to find the answer. Since the age of five, we are taught that 2+2=4. Realistically, and, of course, logically, this can't be mathematically wrong. In fact, any logical person who states that 2+2=4 is false is, in fact, illogical. But what if I said that logically 2+2=5, could this be true? As a teacher of English, it is not only my job to help students think outside the box but also to encourage them to think differently. While it is possible that there are other ways to *prove* how 2+2=5 with a super-long equation, it is not my intention to do so at this time. Read on if you'd like to find out more.

***

Sometimes it's not about finding the "right" answers; sometimes it's about learning how you got to the correct answer. Part of learning is learning from failure. Many of our past presidents, innovators, and scientists failed in at least one point in their lives. The sixteenth president of the United States, Abraham Lincoln, failed as a businessman before becoming president. Even Vincent Van Gogh, who is famous for his paintings, couldn't sell any of them in his early years. In order to succeed, students (and teachers) need to fail to learn. But it's not just learning from failure; it's about learning where the mistake occurred in finding the logical answers. Here are some suggestions that can be modified to help increase authentic student learning.

Find the Logical Explanation for Creative Thinking

With Differentiated Instruction, it's crucial to instill critical thinking skills. Before reading George Orwell's novel *1984* (1948), I introduce my students to critical thinking, which leads to the scaffolding of learning. In order to do so, I begin the class by making a simple statement, "at the age of five, we are taught that 2+2=4." Some students look at me while the others drift away. "However, today, I can prove that 2+2=5." At this point, students begin to stare at me with curiosity and disbelief. In the novel, at one point, the main character, Winston Smith, states that 2+2=5 because "Big Brother" says it's true. To explain how different governments work, I decided to "logically" prove the 2+2 theory to be correct, and so begins my lesson of instruction.

"At the age of five, you are told that 2+2=4, the color red stands for hot, and a radio is not a television. Now what you would say if I could prove that 2+2=5 and, in fact, the color blue stands for hot?" Students begin to talk among themselves and shake their heads in disbelief. Usually, one student will voice an opinion and tell me that I am wrong. I take a quick glance around the room and ask how. At this point, a discussion ensues about what we are taught as infants compared to where we are now.

I stand there listening and focus on their discussion. Without talking, I write 2+2=5 on the board. But instead of saying the word, plus, I use the synonym "and." At this point, I ask my students what this symbol "+" means. Some of the answers:

- A hospital
- Emergency
- A cross
- A plus sign
- Letter "t"
- Intersection

Using what the students state, I begin to write on the board:

$$2+2=5$$
$$2t(2) = 5$$
$$\frac{4t}{4} = \frac{5}{4}$$
$$(5/4 = 1.25)$$
$$t = 1.25$$

Once again, my students were skeptical and said that my equation did not work because my final answer was 1.25. Of course, I knew at least one of my students would call me out.

I explain that I saw the "+" symbol as the letter t and, therefore, look at the problem from a different perspective by multiplying a variable instead of using an addition sign. I tell my student, "you're right." But I checked my work to make sure my answer is correct. Without any more discussion, I write on the board:

$$2 \, (1.25) \, 2 = 5$$
$$2 \, (2.5) = 5$$
$$5 = 5$$

I turn around, place the marker on the board behind me, and walk to the side of the room. I give students a chance to look at the board before saying anything else. My students, even the ones who were staring at their phones in the beginning, were now staring at the whiteboard struggling to figure out what I did. After a few moments, I say, "done" and stop there. One student speaks up and said, "you said 2+2=5, but you wrote 2t which means you are multiplying. How can the 'plus' be the letter 't'?"

With the help of a large group discussion, the questions are formulated to meet the needs of varying levels of learning. While this may not seem like a typical DI lesson, it was broken down into several steps. Part of using DI is not just on assignments, but also within the level of questioning and explaining. I broke down the explanation into steps to prove how 2+2=5.

As stated before, we look at different perspectives. Some students might have seen a letter; I saw it differently. This is similar to the old woman/young woman illusion.

Figure 2. My Wife and My Mother-In-Law, by the cartoonist W. E. Hill, 1915. Retrieved from commons.wikimedia.org

Looking closely at the photo. Some can see the "old woman" almost immediately. On the other hand, with a closer eye, others see the young woman. The illusion of the old woman/young woman is based on one's perspective. By concentrating on one area of the photo, parts of the young woman are visibly seen — for example, the old woman's mouth becomes the young woman's necklace. But by focusing on the picture as a whole, some people see both images simultaneously.

Both of these examples illustrate how one's perspective changes the outlook in situations, similar to what Winston Smith (from Orwell's *1984)* believed. Since he was told 2+2=5, there was no way to dismiss the fact. Sometimes there is a need to view other perspectives to understand the lessons presented to us.

Questions for Further Reflection:

1.   Focusing on all the different perspectives in the classroom, what is one lesson that you can modify to be more creative?

2.   Critical thinking increases student understanding, along with problem-solving capabilities. How might a teacher help students enhance their critical thinking skills daily?

Ch. 4: Collaboration is the Key

Learn to Collaborate with Colleagues

Learning how to differentiate instruction is not just about increasing student awareness. Collaborating with teachers is no different than students collaborating with each other. I think about how I can better help my students succeed, learn, and become focused when I work with other educators. In the article "The Power of Teacher Collaboration," Jones (2014) states, "Successful collaborations happen when teachers work together to share the workload instead of doubling their effort, we teach students to work together and think critically." However, many of us are not using our greatest resources in this profession: each other. Working collaboratively builds relationships with colleagues and raises the culture within the school to increase students' ability to learn.

My co-collaborator and friend, Maggie Maslowski, is also my coworker. For years, she and I have taught the same course. Even though our schedules do not always align to plan together, we find the time to help our students succeed. Maggie and I have different personalities, yet we are able to connect both on a professional level and a personal level. Maggie is more of a "caring" type of person, whereas I am a "take charge" kind of person. When there are times that I cannot stay focused, Maggie is the one who puts things in perspective for me. She understands my accomplishments, my triumphs, and, dare I say, my failures. It's an amazing feeling to know that I have that *one* colleague who knows what I am going through and completely understands it.

From working with Maggie on several projects throughout the years, I began to collaborate with her and other colleagues to create interdisciplinary assignments.

Below are some interdisciplinary units that I created to connect English literature to other courses.

Interdisciplinary Unit 1: Chorus & English

While reading Gabriel Garcia Marquez's *Chronicle of a Death Foretold* (1981), students learn about several characters who all were at fault for the murder of one man. Each character's lie, deceit, and/or knowledge of the crime caused Santiago Nasar's death. During this unit of study, the choir director was working on the musical, *Into the Woods* (Stephen Sondheim, 1987). Each character from the novel was compared to the characters in the musical. I met with the choir director, Tim, before and after school to create a meaningful project to connect the curriculum to our academy focus.

After a few weeks of planning, I came up with a project connecting the two courses. Students were invited to the choir room during class to listen to two select songs from the student performers, where they were asked questions as they stayed in character. The next day we had a forty-five-minute large group class discussion. This all led up to the final project where students applied their knowledge of the extended story, *Metamorphosis by Franz Kafka* (1915). Students were to metamorphosize a character from the story to the similar character from the musical.

To make this project authentic, the students' work, without names, was placed on a website for voting. The top three students received free tickets to the musical. To showcase all projects, they were neatly arranged on two tables covered with a black cloth in the lobby where visitors could see the students' work focusing on authenticity.

Examples of Finished Projects

Abigail — English 2 First Place Winner

Abigail used colored pencils to depict her view of how the beans (that Jack used) transformed into the knives that killed Santiago Nasar. The beans from the musical *Into the Woods* are planted where all the troubles began. Just like in *Chronicle of a Death Foretold*, the trouble started with the knives to represent the "sacrificial" killing of another. The beans metamorphosed into the two knives that killed Santiago Nasar.

Emily — English 2 — Second Place Winner

Here Emily created her metamorphosis by using the character Davina Flor from the novel, *Chronicle of a Death Foretold* and Rapunzel from the musical, *Into the Woods*. Davina is a young girl whose mother tries to protect her from the hands of Santiago Nasar. Just like Davina's mother wants to protect her, the same was true for Rapunzel as she was locked away in a tower to protect her from unwanted love. Emily used these similarities between the two characters to create her own perspective of what Davina and Rapunzel would look like.

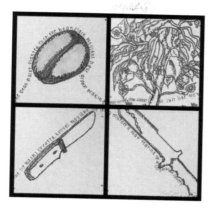

Mateo — English 2 Third Place Winner

Mateo took a different approach to his metamorphosis project; he decided to use the two main objects from both stories. The single bean that Jack traded for his white cow was morphed into the knife that killed Santiago Nasar. The bean created the reason for the giant to climb down the beanstalk. Jack took something from him, so he was determined to get it back. Just like the giant, the Vicario brothers felt that due to their sister's word and disrespect to the family they needed to get something back from Santiago, whether it was the truth or not.

As part of the interdisciplinary unit, students used their creative skills focusing on the Arts & Communication Academy to combine Franz Kafka's "Metamorphosis," Gabriel Garcia Marquez's *Chronicle of a Death Foretold*, and the musical, *Into the Woods*.

Cinderella metamorphosed from a person into birds and, ultimately, into the townspeople. The fact that the decision of one person could change the life of another. The student created four different images that, when placed next to each other, connected. Artist: Kristy K.

Student Interdisciplinary Work: kristenkoppers.wixsite.com/diteaching/interdisciplinary-units

Interdisciplinary Unit 2: Math, History, & English

Combining the scaffolding of lessons and collaboration with other educators, instruction is differentiated through the content that is being learned. With reading literature, it's difficult for students to understand certain concepts while there are other students who are able to grasp the information almost immediately.

"Differentiating instruction may mean teaching the same material to all students using a variety of instructional strategies, or it may require the teacher to deliver lessons at varying levels of difficulty based on the ability of each student" (Wesley, 2014).

My English 2 students read Harper Lee's *To Kill A Mockingbird* (1960) in their freshman year. I utilized their prior knowledge with a different approach, connecting the students to events in the play, *To Kill A Mockingbird*. Based on the book and the Triangle Inequality Theorem, unit objectives were aligned to state standards. However, as an English teacher, I needed some help understanding this theorem to ensure that the connections were valid. My hallmates and counterparts explained the Triangle Inequality Theorem to me. So, with their help, I was able to create an assignment connecting three important characters from the novel to a mathematical equation.

Creating an interdisciplinary lesson

Creating and implementing an interdisciplinary lesson engages students by focusing on critical thinking skills. Based on Harper Lee's novel, *To Kill a Mockingbird*, the readers learn that Tom Robinson, an African American male, is found guilty by his "peers" for the sexual assault of a white woman. The historical background of this book is essential to understanding how African Americans did not receive a fair trial during the pre-Civil Rights Movement. Tom Robinson was accused and, therefore, wrongly convicted and sent to prison. Ultimately, he was unfairly killed (shot) by the prison guards for "trying to escape."

Based on the above information, students used the characters Atticus Finch (Robinson's lawyer), Tom Robinson (the accused), and Bob Ewell (father of the accuser) as the variables. Students first needed to consider, 'is it possible that two people are greater than one **or** can two people be less than one?' To understand this concept, students needed to know and understand the Triangle Inequality Theorem.

The Triangle Inequality Theorem states: the sum of two sides has to be greater than the third in order to form a triangle. An example of the theorem is shown here:

$$3, 4, 5 \qquad 2, 2, 6$$
$$3+4 > 5 \qquad 2+2 \neq 6$$

The Triangle Inequality Theorem was then applied it to the characters in *To Kill A Mockingbird*. Due to the structure of the novel, only three of the characters were essential to the assignment.

Atticus Finch (a)

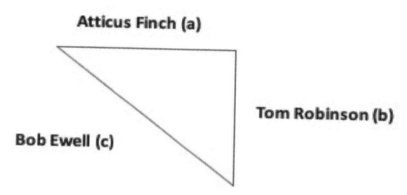

Tom Robinson (b)

Bob Ewell (c)

Side (a) represented Atticus Finch, side (b) represented Tom Robinson, and side (c) represented Bob Ewell. The triangle itself represents society. If the Triangle Inequality Theorem is valid, then the sum of two sides (a. Atticus Finch and b. Tom Robinson) is greater than the third side (c. Bob Ewell). Both Finch and Robinson are not strong to stand alone; however, together they are greater than Ewell. Atticus Finch was viewed poorly by society because he was defending an African American male (Tom Robinson). The previous statement: 'is it possible that two people are greater than one **or** can two people be less than one' is debatable based on proving if the theorem is valid or not. Students were allowed to decide whether it is possible or not with proof from the novel while still connecting their answer to the theorem.

The assignment began:

> *Write a synthesis paragraph in 9 - 12 sentences answering the question below. The essay needs to follow proper, formal MLA guidelines. Before beginning to write the essay, you will need to answer the following question: Is Bob Ewell greater or less than Atticus Finch and Tom Robinson within society? In order to answer this question, you will need to use prior knowledge of Harper Lee's novel, To Kill A Mockingbird, along with the play adaptation of the book using the Triangle Inequality Theorem.*

Now, as an English teacher, I would normally focus on the literary side rather than on the mathematical side. However, I did not want the students to believe that I was "throwing in" an interdisciplinary connection; rather I wanted to show them that connections can be 50/50 of the assignment. I studied up on the Triangle Inequality Theorem to ensure that I knew how to connect the two courses. As part of the interdisciplinary connection, the mathematics teacher reviewed the theorem and followed with the characters for a, b, and c in her class.

The benefits of interdisciplinary lessons connect teachers sharing a common goal. The goals range from state standards to focusing on student achievement through various educational skills. Students have the opportunity to think critically from one class to the other while still reflecting on the lessons learned in each class.

Teacher collaboration is an intricate part of education; it shows students a positive connection among teachers. While some schools provide common times for teachers to collaborate, scheduling in other schools prohibit this opportunity. As a result, many teachers choose not to create interdisciplinary assignments.

Lily Jones, a K-1 teacher, understands the importance of teacher collaboration. In her article, "The Power of Teacher Collaboration" (2014), she states that, "the relationships you build with colleagues aren't just good for your mental well-being; they're also the foundation of collaboration that can result in increased student achievement" (1.3).

However, collaboration does not happen overnight. In fact, it takes time as "collaboration begins with finding time to connect with colleagues, to share thoughts, and provide support" (Jones, 2014). The first step to create an effective interdisciplinary unit is being willing to give up some time to share ideas with other educators.

Maggie and I continually build interconnecting units. We teach the same course, and we connect our lessons by using Lync (a form of Skype) to teach, discuss, and communicate. At one point two years ago, she and I teamed up with another teacher, Kevin Michaels, who was teaching Health, to create a triad through Lync. Our English classes were reading Charlotte Perkins Gilman's short story, "The Yellow Wallpaper" (1892), while Kevin was teaching our students about mental health disorders and illnesses. Any one of us could teach the class even though we were in three different classrooms in three different parts of the building. By the end of the unit, students wrote an essay on one of the characters from the short story and incorporated one of the mental health disorders or illnesses learned in Health.

Each of us was responsible for checking for accuracy of students' essays. The English teachers evaluated the writing process, while the Health teacher checked for the connections of the mental illness in relation to the story. Teacher collaboration does not have to take weeks to implement. A lesson could be created via a few emails to finalize the plans. It could be just a one-day lesson that teachers connect through collaboration. There is a link between teacher collaboration and differentiated instruction. Teaming up with colleagues to focus on student achievement results knowing and learning the students' ability. Earlier on, I focused on one of the ways to DI teaching by knowing the student's interest.

Creating PLNs: What are They?

I learned about PLNs (Professional Learning Network) and how I could use social media to connect with other educators across the nation, and even across the world. I found myself starting to tweet simple ideas focused on my school, but soon, I joined Twitter chats with participants who were educators, administrators, and even consultants. These chats led me to attend the first What Great Educators Do Differently conference held in Illinois. When I first signed up to attend, I wanted to know what these educators knew that I didn't. I knew I was a good educator, but was I great? At the very start by meeting Todd Whitaker, Jeff Zoul, and Jimmy Casas, I knew this was no ordinary conference. In fact, little did I know that this conference was the start of changing my educational perspective. This conference gave me a whole new insight to differentiating the way I teach.

> It was great to know that even though I was in the company of some of the best, I was equal to them.

After two days, my PLN grew from just a few local teachers to quite a bit nationally. Paul Solarz, author of *Learn Like a Pirate* (2015), was one of the teachers that I met who focuses on his students learning abilities. It was great to know that even though I was in the company of some of the best, I was equal to them. Now I have to admit that I began writing this before reading his book (sorry Paul); I noticed his section on Peer Collaboration (the "P" in Pirate). While reading his book, I was amazed how this section described collaborating with students more so than colleagues. Even though I work with my students and create student-led classrooms (which Solarz also mentions in his book), I never thought about collaborating as much as he has with students. One of his sections in the chapter "We're in this Together" got me thinking that it's not the teacher vs. students. "We rely on one another as we work together" (Solarz, 2015, p. 39). Solarz is right — we, teachers and students, are in this together. Students need to learn from me as well as I do from them. Since then, I have been collaborating with my students to create a better culture within the classroom. Their input is just as important as mine or other colleagues.

So how does a PLN fit into Differentiated Instruction? PLN means Personal Learning Network. PLN does not have to come from other educators; in fact, building a PLN with students is an ideal way for them to feel like they are a part of the class. By including students in creating lessons, maintaining classroom management, or even having them create discussions within the class, a PLN is created. This is why we, as teachers, need to shift our thinking in the classroom.

To increase our educator-based PLN, Maggie and I created a Twitter chat by reaching out to colleagues monthly. Our chat, #HSEDUCHAT, provided discussions on various topics related to education, motivation, collaboration, and more.

Educator Connection
Joy Kirr (Twitter @joykirr)
Thomas Middle School (Arlington Heights, Illinois)
ELA, Grade 4

At the end of each quarter, I sit down with my students, one-on-one, and we talk about their learning from the past seven or eight weeks. Ultimately, we have to come up with one letter grade that represents learning they've shown. This one little letter is all they get for their work, but that's how the system is for me at this moment in time.

These conferences are my most stressful time of each quarter, and also my favorite. They're stressful because I need to make sure I have time to see each student, and I hope to goodness that they're not absent the day they were scheduled. They're also stressful because I then have to enter that one grade in the online gradebook, and I worry about parent reactions.

These conferences are also my favorite time of each quarter. This is a result of the conversations we have, the learning that is demonstrated and celebrated, and the reflections and goal setting.

Here are some tidbits from this past quarter. All names are changed and do not resemble the child's name.

- Abby's goal for next quarter is to ask more questions. She didn't know where an assignment was, and was too nervous to ask me. ME. I wonder how she functions in other classes.

- Bill's goal for next quarter is to set his alarm on his phone, so he remembers to read every day after school. He went to his locker and set it right then.

- Cliff realized, although he's doing very well academically, that he has a tough time with theme and the author's message. He decided he's going to write about the theme of everything he reads in class and at home from now on.

- Donny is proud that he's now reading at home and that he found a genre he enjoys (nonfiction).

- Edgar thought he should get a "D" in class because he never reads at home. We had a great discussion about how reading habits affect comprehension, but that I don't think habits should belong in a grade. It turns out we agreed on a "C" because his comprehension was in the 70% range. He asked, "If I read more, will it go up?" I gotta tell him that the only thing that helps improve reading comprehension is more reading.

- Frank revised, then revised, then revised once again to improve the grammar in his writing the week before we met. His new goal? --> Revise as soon as he gets feedback!

- George, once again, admits to playing video games all afternoon and evening. Talking with him helps me know that I can NOT do it all alone. It also helps reaffirm that we should be reading (books of students' choices) in class every day.
- Helga's goal for next quarter is to stay away from distracting friends during independent reading time.
- Kelly realized (without my help) that she is distracting other students when they work in a group! Her new goal is to focus on getting the task accomplished when she works with friends.
- Leo was nervous about his meeting with me. He came and said, "I'm nervous." It turns out that he was hyper-focused on one part of the grade. When we looked over the other evidence, he said, "I'm not as nervous anymore." We discussed averaging points in the gradebook versus taking the evidence for what it is, and he was happy he had revised his writing.
- Molly's new goal is to head to our class website reading Challenge page to look through the myriad lists of books and create a large list for herself so she can

begin to choose what to read on her own (instead of coming to me each time she finishes a book).

- Nick thought he should get a "D" because of his behavior in class. We then discussed how behavior will impact his learning at some point, but for now, the evidence for his academics shows he's in the "B" range. We then talked about how his behavior might be impacting OTHER students' learning...

- Olga's new goal is to stop doodling during class work time. She didn't do as well as she'd hoped this past quarter and blames it on "not getting down to work."

- Patrick told me he really wants to change seats, so he's away from a certain someone who distracts him.

Those are the stories I remember offhand, without going back into my notes. When I feel as if my class is slipping away from me (let's call it "spring fever"), I can go back to these conversations and realize that we do have a connection, and we can have discussions about what's going right, and where we can improve.

Questions for Further Reflection:

1.   Student-teacher collaboration is an important model to use for students to take ownership. What can you do to change a lesson to give students more ownership?

2.   Creating an interdisciplinary unit is an authentic way to collaborate with colleagues. Focus on a unit, a lesson, or an assignment that you can collaborate on with colleagues or students. How might you introduce the idea of collaboration?

Ch. 5: Making Work Authentic

Students want to take ownership of their own work. They want to feel as if what their learning is relevant to them. Students are presented with real-world problems to think critically while working collaboratively with their group. Problem-Based Learning or Project-Based Learning assignments increase engagement in the classroom.

Problem-Based Learning

The Problem-Based Learning (PBL) assignment gives students the opportunity to take ownership of their work. Because PBL focuses on finding solutions to problems around the world, I want the students to be proud of their work by making it their own. One way is to give them the chance to become the teachers as we become the learners. Students focus on what they want to learn to challenge themselves. Students were grouped together by similar interests.

I didn't just want my students to submit work for me; I wanted them to understand that their work has meaning to others. Using the *Weebly* web authoring site, I created a free teacher account, controlling usernames, passwords, and overall the entire account to enable monitoring student contributions. Students were able to use the site and work at their own level. Although all my students were ultimately creating a similar website, they were given ownership of how to create and maintain it.

Working on the Problem-Based Learning, I invited teachers, our Board of Education members, administrators, guests, and political partners to work with the student groups one-on-one. The guests were not there to watch or supervise; rather they were there to help educate as they worked with the students as a member of the group. They were part of the project creating a truly collaborative partnership.

The first part of the assignment was to create a homepage on the *Weebly* website with project descriptions and descriptors of what the student should do. The information on the site helped them to review the guidelines while working on their project. The project descriptions focused on where the students should be heading as well as examples to help guide them as they worked in groups, or as individuals. In the end, they created a presentation based on their webpage to share with their classmates.

Genius Hour

kristenkoppers.wixsite.com/diteaching/genius-hour

When I first heard of the concept of Genius Hour, I thought it was merely another fleeting strategy. Joy Kirr's book, *Shift This* (2017) explains how teachers gradually implement authentic learning that is student-driven: "Genius Hour is authentic, student-driven, and inquiry-driven," (Kirr, 2017, p. 137). It is about students finding a passion for their learning to create authentic work. "This dedicated time (no matter how long) is for students to take control of their own learning" (Kirr, 2017, p. 137). I've been learning about Genius Hour (GH) from several of my peers through my PLN .but never really caught onto it. Instead, I continued to modify my PBL unit each year. After the third year, I realized that I needed a change in how students were able to choose their own topics. The Genius Hour project allowed students to not only choose their own project topic but also their own way of presenting it.

At the USM Summer Spark Conference in 2017, I wanted to learn more about Genius Hour and how closely it related to PBLs. Joy Kirr, a middle school teacher and author, presented on both topics at the conference. As I listened, I took notes, searched the internet for examples, and focused on what she was saying.

Interdisciplinary PBL/GH

Some teachers refer to individual authentic learning as Passion Projects, Problem-Based Learning, or Project-Based Learning. Even though the terms vary, the idea of Genius Hour is consistent across them. Students can choose a project that focuses on researching a topic of interest to them. By including a student-led project, I try to focus on gradual shifts in my lessons. I changed the wording from Project-Based Learning to Genius Hour. However, Kirr notes "gradual" does not mean that teachers stop what they are doing to teach something new — what I tried to do. We need to make slight changes. This is something I needed to focus on more as I realize that my "shifts" were not gradual.

So, instead of just getting rid of all the work I put into my PBL projects, I used the same idea but changed the outcome (a gradual shift). Researching during the summer months, I tried to find ideas more aligned for high school rather than elementary school. I still wanted to keep the rigor of the assessment but also give students the benefit of understanding the project. While I still needed to perfect this idea (as teachers we know we continually adjust our lessons), I found when implementing the concept, the students were more involved in a project than the previous years.

Learning to differentiate instruction with students can range from a large group activity to individualized lesson plans. The benefits of this method increase student engagement and interest while they learn how to challenge themselves. Three of my students enjoy drawing; they combined their interests to create a Genius Hour on "How to Create a Comic Book." One day a week was set aside for working on their own ideas. With a few guidelines, students were in charge of their own learning.

Educator Connection
Melissa Pilakowski (Twitter @mpilakow)
Valentine High School (Valentine, Nebraska)
ELA, Grades 11-12

In video games, players move at their own pace, replay levels until they pass, and take different routes. What if we could make our teaching and classes more like a video game?

You can through quest-based learning.

Putting video game mechanics into your classroom is more than a gimmick. It's an extremely effective way to level up your current situation, especially if you're already using components of blended learning. Quest-Based Learning (QBL) combines gamification and blended learning into a motivational system for students.

In QBL, lessons and activities are plotted out on a visual map for students to move through at their own speed. My favorite platform for this style of teaching is Classcraft, but it can also be achieved through DeckToys, Sutori, Google Suite, or other platforms.

QBL uses so many of the same mechanics as video games, and that's what makes it so successful. For example:

Self-Pacing. In video games, players move at their own chosen pace. This is the same with Quest-Based Learning. I still have deadlines that students need to meet for completing quests, but students can progress through them at the personal pace that works best. This promotes the concept of flow (Csikszentmihalyi, 1997), where students are moving at the right pace that challenges them without challenging them too much or not enough.

Mastery. Video games let players attempt a level again and again until they're successful. Again, same with Quest-Based Learning. Some platforms, such as Classcraft and DeckToys, allow teachers to prevent a student from moving on until they've mastered the material or skills.

Choice. Quest-Based Learning is all about giving students choice, whether that's choice in the product they make, choice in the articles they read, or choice in the method of learning (such as video, reading, or podcast). Some teachers also add "side quests"; in video games, these are optional quests that players can take to explore more or earn points. This same concept can be applied to the classroom. Side quests can provide reinforcement, review, or enrichment of what's being learned in the classroom.

Other Game Mechanics. Many teachers add other mechanics to increase student interest and engagement to discover what happens.

Quest-Based Learning doesn't mean completely independent learning. Most days, I lead a mini-lesson or review with students to introduce new topics or address misconceptions students have. There are days that we have whole-class activities, such as discussions, peer-review, or simulations.

Fostering a Quest-Based Learning classroom has enabled me to work more closely with students, leading to more small-group and one-on-one time rather than full-group time. Plus, students are more engaged and more responsible for their learning. For me, Quest-Based Learning has been a complete win in my classroom.

Educator Connection
Tom Spall (Twitter @Tommyspall)
Alton Elementary School (Brenham, Texas)
STEM, Grade 4

A couple of years ago, our district's instructional technology specialist team started an initiative to train teachers in conducting PBL instruction within their classrooms. This initiative, conducted during the beginning of the summer with selected teachers taken from an application process, was called WOW Academy.

This is a four-day, intensive, hands-on, collaborative academy that spent the better part of the first day training teachers in all things PBL: implementation, pedagogy, history, and practicality. The first three of the four days we were working as a team building a unit where we focused on actual grade level content while running the academy as an actual PBL experience. Together in our teams, we created a driving question, utilized technology, collaborated together to explore, created and organized our content, and focused on a grade-level-specific objective.

On the last day, we presented our findings in the auditorium to an audience of our peers, administration, and community members. Learning about PBL in this way allowed our teachers to experience it both as teachers and students. Upon completion of the WOW Academy, teachers were much more capable of running PBL instruction within their actual classrooms during the next school year. We were to take these newly acquired strategies, along with an awarded class Chromebook cart, back to our classrooms to fully integrate with our instruction and curriculum.

I participated in the WOW academy during its second year of implementation. After going through the four-day academy, I began the next school year (2013-2014) more prepared to conduct PBL instruction with my fourth-grade students. I started right at the beginning of the year with introducing my students to a full classroom set of Chromebooks, their district Chrome accounts, and the full array of G Suite applications/tools.

The first driving question I created for my students centered around them, introducing themselves to the class. These introductions involved researching their own family trees, traditions, and hobbies, by using Chromebooks and Google apps. By using Google Slides, Draw, and Docs, they created pamphlets, presentations, posters, infographics, and family tree diagrams to present. These "All About Me" introductions were presented in the library in front of the entire class, invited parents, and our administration. This was an excellent introduction to both PBL instruction and their Google Suite (G-Suite).

Throughout the year during the exploration phases of our PBLs, I started incorporating Genius Hour opportunities into my instructional time. I learned all about Genius Hour opportunities for student enrichment/engagement from Chris Kesler (@iamkesler) when he spoke at the 2013 Edcamp

Waller Conference in Texas. Since my students were already familiar with the Chromebooks and G-Suite tools, we took the opportunity to start exploring with Google Search, Gmail (which at the time, students weren't really using yet across the district), Calendars, Maps, Forms, Sheets, and other Google apps/tools.

They started creating "Interest Projects" in their free time (upon completion of daily assignments and class work) about topics for which they were passionate. They would research, explore, and create using the knowledge and technology readily available for them in class. I soon had students coming into my room way before school began, during lunch and recess, staying after school, and spending independent weekend time working on these passion projects. My Genius Hour turned into Genius Hours, which then turned into a morning collaboration time before school, called "Coffee Break."

I was no longer in control of dictating when and where our classroom learning happened. The students' work was authentic, collaborative, and exciting. The best part about implementing both PBL and Genius Hour into my instruction is that my students wanted to come to school because they were passionate about learning, and they continued to grow and learn in and out of the classroom setting.

Questions for Further Reflection:

1. Authentic learning assists students in being able to problem solve real-life experiences. They also become engaged in their own learning. In what way can you use authentic learning in your classroom to engage students?

2. In order to increase critical thinking skills while using authentic learning, how can social issues connect with what students are learning in the classroom?

3. This chapter of the book focuses on authentic learning, in what way can you implement a Genius Hour type project into the classroom?

Ch. 6: Motivating the "Unmotivated"

While I wish there was a magic wand or a "sure thing" to motivate all students, there is not. Yet, I find different ways of motivating a percentage of the unmotivated students. Just as the title of the book states, we need to use differentiated instruction in the teaching profession, including ways we motivate students.

Every year I teach anywhere from 27-32 students during one class period. While I can get most of them interested in the material, there are a few that I cannot reach (for various reasons). I used to want to win this fight, but I found that it increased my anxiety and made me tired every day. Like many teachers, we instill respect and discipline within the classroom. However, what we tend to forget, and I know that I have, is that times have changed. We cannot teach like were taught.

I've also come to realize that my students all do not learn the same way. So how is it that I can get the one student to read a novel senior year, who hasn't picked up a book in his previous three years? Just like what many teachers do — I get to know my students. I found out what their interests are, what they liked to do, and learned about them as people, not just as a student. I wanted them to feel like part of the class, rather than just another student on the roster.

During classroom discussions, at times, we become "unfocused" and start to discuss current news, sharing family or childhood stories and memories, or interject a little piece of information that might be irrelevant to the lesson. Still, students are engaged.

When it comes time for the novel unit, I give a historical viewpoint, not only about the novel but also about the author. Using this information, I start to connect the novel to the students. Focusing on Kurt Vonnegut's *Slaughterhouse Five*, students learn about the author's past as a soldier, his life before writing, and his connection to the storyline. The novel's title alone creates curiosity. Students believe the book is about slaughtering five people, and so the conversation begins. Just like the PBL unit, I ask students open-ended questions relating to the novel. The key is to bring them into the conversation.

While working on a group project on how to Motivate the Unmotivated, I came across Larry Ferlazzo's article, "Strategies for Helping Students Motivate Themselves" (2015). I find that teaching in a high school setting is more complicated than other grades (granted, high school and college teaching are the only two levels that I have taught). Yet, I feel, at this age, the students are more independent than their younger counterparts.

What really struck me as interesting in Ferlazzo's article was that "providing students with freedom of choice is one strategy for promoting learner autonomy." This allows the students the opportunity to govern their own learning while increasing their motivation to learn. Differentiated Instruction does not have to be teacher-led, where assignments are created and lessons are taught. Because there is some type of solution to the problem, student-led work automatically creates differentiation. "Both teachers and students should become progressively more able to support increasing academic success" (Tomlinson et al., 2013).

After fifteen plus years of teaching, I thought I knew how to teach and in what ways to motivate students. However, two years ago, I implemented the idea of choice. During semester 1, we spent time writing, revising, and proofreading different types of essays focusing on content, grammar, and structure. During semester 2, students had the opportunity to choose to complete a formal essay following all requirements or creating a multimedia video essay speaking their work, instead of writing it. While this may sound easy to some, it is, in fact, a little harder, as students still need to write a rough draft first, which focuses on structure and content. Students still needed quotes written out in the video as part of the necessary support. Depending on time and on the assignment, I have given a third option where students can present their essay to the class verbally, accompanied by a PowerPoint or Google Slide presentation.

Let's face it — students do not learn the same and neither do we. Even if we were to put all the math teachers in one room, there would be different abilities, learning patterns, and different styles of teaching. We need to address this kind of differentiation with our students. DI focuses on altering teaching to meet the needs of *all* students.

Educator Connection
Maggie Maslowski
(Twitter @MaggieMaslowski)
Joliet West High School (Joliet, Illinois)
ELA, Grades 9 – 12

Why are some students "good" at school while others are "bad?" As a parent, how can we motivate a child to do well in school? As an educator, how do you encourage all of our students to follow teacher guidelines, procedures, and expectations?

Years ago, it was just assumed that all students do as they are told, and school is an obligation. Times have changed. People change and evolve. Therefore, schools need to change, and that means educators need to truly redefine how their classrooms look and feel.

I taught at a private school for a few years and was told to instill discipline and give out harsh punishments for misbehavior and missing work. If a student wanted to redo an assignment, the policy was to only give them partial credit. When I began teaching at a public school, I noticed other extreme rules such as not giving full credit for late work, not allowing redoes on assignments, giving zeros for plagiarism, and so on.

None of these felt right to me, yet that's what everyone was doing, so it was expected.

Then, I became a mother...and my children grew into school-age children. That's when I had my "aha moments." That's when I started attending conferences of my own choosing and learning more about the profession.

Being an educator mom forced me to self-reflect on my own practices. I quickly realized what I wanted my sons to experience in school and how I would need to change my own classroom environment to provide a learning experience that was effective, fair, and compassionate.

I wanted my children to enjoy school and to love learning as I do. And, I wanted my own students to feel that same way. Well, it was time for a change. Slowly, I began to see my students as my own children. I stopped focusing on rules and began focusing on *them,* and what would propel them to succeed.

Angela Maiers inspired me with her "You Matter" message, and my way of teaching changed dramatically. Dave Burgess's *Teach Like a Pirate* (2012) message also helped ignite my passion for a different type of classroom, one that I would be willing to have my children attend and one that I believe would motivate all students.

Here's what I started modifying to motivate my students:

<u>No talk of rules or procedures the first days of school</u>. Instead of expecting them to misbehave, I focus on expecting the best out of my students and don't mention rules. I teach at a high school, which means that the first day, many students sit through period after period listening to teachers dictate rules and procedures to them. I want to make a positive first impression with students learning about me and having the chance to learn about them. So, we play a game of Truths and Lies. I start off with sharing some photos and statements of my family, hobbies, and travels. Then, I ask the students to decide which ones are true and which ones aren't. It's a fun way for them to get to know their teacher. Then, I give students time to write down three statements about themselves, making sure that one is false. While they do that, I walk around and talk to the students and put their names to their faces. When it's time to share their Two Truths and a Lie, the students have an opportunity to learn about their classmates.

I want them to leave my class the first day knowing that I'm the teacher who wants to learn about them just as much as I want them to learn about me and the curriculum of the school year. I don't pass out a course syllabus with rules and procedures.

Do you know that each year I have written fewer and referrals, yet I have students on my roster who are considered regulars in the dean's office? I remember a conversation with a dean who came into my room and asked me what I'm doing differently. I asked him what he meant, and he told me that I have a large group of students who are in his office regularly, yet he hasn't seen a referral from me all year. The dean is shocked that students behaved in my class and not in others. I told him that I don't focus on rules, and instead focus on relationships and getting to know the students. When students know they matter, they return that respect to you.

<u>Focus more on students</u>. I encourage my students to design our classroom. During the first few weeks of school, students create posters about themselves, and we post them on the walls. The classroom is OURS, not just mine. What I absolutely LOVE about this poster sharing is that I see students come into class and just walk around the room, learning about their classmates. I have about 150 students each year, so I try to put up about 5-10 new posters every few days so that students can learn about different students without being overwhelmed with a large poster wall all at once. The posters usually have a small photo of the student, likes, favorites, goals, and accomplishments. Students feel pride, especially when classmates ask them about something they shared on their post

I start class with desks organized in tables and allow students to decide where they feel comfortable sitting. We worked on grants to purchase other furniture the students chose and create an alternative learning environment. So, yes, we have a couch, coffee table, a rug, bean bag chair, and several lounge chairs. Students have a choice where to sit, and they work productively. The focus is on providing a comfortable learning environment, where creativity, productivity, and success are invited.

No homework. I received criticism for this one. Many of my colleagues thought I was crazy, but I refused to give students work to take home. Many students didn't have time to do it or didn't have help at home to finish it. I wanted my classroom to be filled with learning, where I was there to support students. If it was important, assignments were done in class. And, because we used our class time effectively and efficiently, many students went home to work harder by revising their work and finding creative learning projects.

Focus on Learning, not on Grading. We all learn from experience and by making mistakes. Yet, in school, we often assess students on their first attempt and then average that into their final grade. Students don't believe it until they see that their formative work doesn't affect their grade. Then, I find that they spend time working on these assignments and learning activities to refine their skills. They do NOT get any points for their efforts. Yet, they realize on their own that practice does become rewarding when they successfully accomplish a summative learning activity or assignment. To see the spark in students, instead of them just doing something to get points, truly shows me why I became a teacher. And, that's what I want for my own children. All kids deserve this type of learning — a genuine learning experience without consequences but instead yields great success when accomplished.

Always believe in your students and NEVER give up on them. I've taught the repeater courses for years and have high success rates. I don't just pass these students. I actually hold very high expectations, and I work 1:1 with them as much as I can. I do not grade incomplete work, or that doesn't meet the basic standards. I return it and guide students to successfully accomplish the task.

By showing that I believe and support them through their revision process, students work harder. Many students come into my class already feeling they are bad, and already shut down even before starting. When I continue to encourage them without punishing them, they often realize that trying to work in my class will benefit them. Then, when they see success, a magical light goes off.

Questions for Further Reflection:

1.   Many students feel disengaged in class for several reasons. What are some ways that you motivate students in class?

2.   As an educator, we know that students have a sense of control or opinion about lessons. In what way can students feel that they have ownership in the lessons?

Ch. 7: Ways to Differentiate Learning

In school, students are taught memory techniques called acronyms to help them remember concepts. For instance, to remember the planets in order, students are taught *My Very Educated Mother Just Served Us Nine Pizzas* to recall Mercury, Venus, Earth, Mars, Jupiter, Saturn, Uranus, Neptune, and recently the dwarf planet, Pluto. However, if a teacher were to ask how to spell *principal*, many might spell it with an -le instead of an -al. To remember the correct spelling, some would say that a principal is your "pal."

But what happens when students reach higher grades such as high school? As students become older, these simple techniques are not as useful as they once were in elementary school. While attending graduate school, one of the books that we read was *Made to Stick* by Chip Heath and Dan Heath (2006). Their focus, "Why Some Ideas Survive and Others Die," is an exciting approach to education. Even though their book focuses on businesses, their work also applies to education. The first chapter, "Simple," revolves around the simplicity of finding the one idea that works. Politicians often take the "simple" out of context and try to create a ten-step problem with ten "great" steps, instead of one simple step.

In fact, it's not just politicians who do this, but also educators. With writing a simple expository essay for class, an English teacher might give the students a choice by creating an outline, drawing a mind map, or even brainstorming ideas to use as a prewriting technique. While doing this, students might become unfocused or confused. Writing an essay is not as easy as adding 2 plus 2 together. Truthfully, due to the subjective nature of essay writing, the writing is more at the teacher's discretion.

For students to have a simple, yet concrete (which is also a chapter in *Made to Stick*) idea of how to write an introduction, I provide a skeleton outline of essay writing:

I.   Introduction
    A.   Hook
    B.   Broad Information
    C.   Topic
    D.   Thesis statement

Even this type of set-up causes confusion. To make things as concrete and straightforward as possible, I give my students a sentence formula that will help the process of writing become a little easier.

Example:

First sentence: Hook of the paper (attention-grabber)

Second sentence: Explain the attention-getter (in writer's own words)

Third sentence: Explanation of the second sentence; begins to introduce the broad information on the topic

Fourth sentence: Continue with broad information

Fifth sentence: Elaborate on broad information

Sixth sentence: Continuation of broad information leading into the topic

Seventh sentence: Topic information (think what specifically is the paper about?)

Eighth sentence: Continue elaboration about the topic

Ninth sentence: End topic and lead into thesis idea

Tenth sentence: Thesis statement

While some might think that ten sentences for an introduction are too much, this is dependent on the type of essay as well as the information needed. Everything can be scaled down; however, this model provides the student with a concrete goal. Simplicity does not necessarily equate to brevity. The simplicity of this model focuses on giving students a template to use and being able to alter it. The fact that the outline is concrete encourages students to reuse it multiple times and for multiple classes as needed. Teaching students different ways of how to format a paper is just one way to differentiate writing.

Chip and Dan Heath explain that concrete ideas are not necessarily taken at face value by most people. "We need ways to help people test our ideas for themselves — a 'try before you buy' philosophy for the world of ideas" (Heath & Heath, 2007, p. 114). Many educators are reluctant to embrace new ideas because they are not sure if they will work. With this in mind, it's essential to find out from the students what works and what doesn't.

> Instead of changing the way we teach writing, why not focus on helping the way students think and learn?

Instead of changing the way we teach writing, why not focus on helping the way students think and learn? If you asked me to recite William Shakespeare's "To Be or Not to Be" speech from *Hamlet* (1609), I could because I recited the words over and over again during my sophomore year of high school. I was not able to remember the soliloquy in its entirety. However, if I studied and memorized each line one at a time, I would be able to recite the entire monologue.

The more students can recite information, the better they will remember it for years to come, or at least this is what we were told to believe. The truth is that just memorizing material does not really help the students.

This reminds me of the history courses that I have taken throughout college. Even though I have taken several courses on US History, I could not remember all the US Presidents in order. It wasn't until my trip to Monticello in Virginia that I learned that Adams, Jefferson, and Monroe all died on July 4 (the second, third, and fifth presidents of the United States of America). Even though I may not remember all the presidents in order, I learned more about the early presidents through concrete and simple information over any memorization technique. This is what students need today. The possibility that all students can learn the same or even memorize all the facts is not true. Remembering all the planets in order followed a mnemonic device: *My Very Educated Mother Just Served Us Nine Pizzas* (Mercury, Venus, Earth, Mars, Jupiter, Saturn, Uranus, Neptune, and Pluto). Teachers have been applying DI work for years without realizing it. Just by the mnemonic device used to remember the planets, it is altering the way students (I) learn.

When we think of Differentiated Instruction, some educators might cringe at the thought of additional lessons. However, that's not what Differentiated Instruction is about. Differentiated Instruction is not about making more work for the teacher or the student. It's about adjusting the way we teach to meet the needs of each student.

Don't think of it as separating all students or creating one lesson plan for many. It's about assessing student needs throughout the year. One assignment can be adjusted for some. But look past the lessons and assignments and think about how you can differentiate the unit. Instead of teaching a novel with PowerPoints or handouts, change the way the novel is taught.

Questions for Further Reflection:

1.   By properly using Differentiating Instruction in the classroom, all students should be able to learn based on their own ability. Think of an assignment that you give students. How might you be able to differentiate it to meet the needs of all students?

2.   Sometimes simplicity is better in education. Simplifying an assignment or lesson allows students to understand the end goal. Before beginning any unit, lesson, or assignment, how do you determine the end goal?

Conclusion

What we need to remember as educators is that we support the success of our students. Through the use of Differentiated Instruction, it's possible to meet the different learning styles of all students without creating individualized lesson plans. I've learned to focus on students following the precept "one size does not fit all." Students come from a variety of backgrounds and cultures and have varied learning abilities, so we cannot think "one size" can fit all.

We must not forget that it's all about focusing on the needs of the students. Differentiated Instruction recognizes we have a diverse classroom of learners, and we need to help them process the information not just complete an assignment. While we are still meeting the needs of our students, as teachers, we are innovative thinkers seeking multiple ways to motivate our students. I found that motivating students takes time, but finding the right way to implement DI that works creates a positive atmosphere for students to learn.

The strategy allows students to be in control of their learning. Students want to learn, and they want to be able to connect ideas that they've learned previously. Differentiated Instruction is about connecting the concepts learned in school while being able to use that information. No longer will students say, "Why do I have to learn this?" but instead, "Now I know why I have to learn this."

References

Csikszentmihalyi, M. (1997). Finding flow: The psychology of engagement with everyday life. New York, NY: Basic Books.

Ferlazzo, L. (2015, March 25). Strategies for Helping Students Motivate Themselves. Edutopia. Retrieved from https://www.edutopia.org/blog/strategies-helping-students-motivate-themselves-larry-ferlazzo

Heath, C., & Heath, D. (2007). Made to stick. New York, NY: Random House.

Jones, L. (2014, July 18). "The Power of Teacher Collaboration." Retrieved December 14, 2018, from Teaching Channel website: https://www.teachingchannel.org/blog/2014/07/18/power-of-teacher-collaboration-nea/

Kirr, J. (2017). Shift This. San Diego, CA: Dave Burgess Consulting.

Miller, M., & Keeler, A. (2017). Ditch that homework. San Diego, CA: Dave Burgess Consulting.

Solarz, P. (2015). Learn like a pirate. San Diego, CA: Dave Burgess Consulting.

The Cornell Note-taking System. (n.d.). Retrieved April 13, 2019, from Cornell University website: lsc.cornell.edu/notes.html

Tomlinson, C. A., Moon, T., & Imbeau., M. (2013, September). "Assessment and Student Success in a Differentiated Classroom." Retrieved April 9, 2019, from ASCD website: http://www.ascd.org/ASCD/pdf/siteASCD/publications/assessment-and-di-whitepaper.pdf

Wesley, C. (2014, October 1). "What is differentiated instruction? Examples of How to Differentiate Instruction in the Classroom." Retrieved April 13, 2019, from Concordia University-Portland website: https://education.cu-portland.edu/blog/classroom-resources/examples-of-differentiated-instruction/

About the Author

Kristen Koppers is a blogger, presenter, self-published author, and high school educator as well as an adjunct professor at a local junior college. She has been teaching for more than fifteen years and is currently teaching high school English Language Arts in Illinois. She was a Google Level 1 Certified Educator and National Board-Certified Teacher. Kristen has a Master's degree in English and a second Master's degree in Education Administration.

Kristen wrote the book *Differentiated Instruction in the Teacher Profession* as a way to share her ideas of how to use Differentiated Instruction inside the classroom. As an educator, it is important to find innovative ways to meet the needs of students. Kristen is often on Twitter (@Mrs_Koppers) participating in chats and collaborating with other educators. It's easy to share DI ideas on Twitter (#DITeaching). kristenkoppers.wixsite.com/koppers

Other EduMatch Books

Journey to The "Y" in You by Dene Gainey

This book started as a series of separate writing pieces that were eventually woven together to form a fabric called The Y in You. The question is, "What's the 'why' in you?" Why do you? Why would you? Why should you? Through the pages in this book, you will gain the confidence to be you, and understand the very power in what being you can produce.

The Teacher's Journey by Brian Costello

Follow the Teacher's Journey with Brian as he weaves together the stories of seven incredible educators. Each step encourages educators at any level to reflect, grow, and connect. The Teacher's Journey will ignite your mind and heart through its practical ideas and vulnerable storytelling.

In Other Words by Rachelle Dene Poth

Teddy Roosevelt once said, "I am a part of everything I have read." When Rachelle read his quote, it greatly resonated with her because of her love of quotes and the impact they can have in our lives. In Other Words is a book full of inspirational and thought-provoking quotes that have pushed her thinking, inspired her, and given her strength when she needed it

Math SEAL (curriculum) by Tenickia Polk

Math SEALs is a great tool for math intervention programs, after-school programs, and summer camps for students in grades 3-6. The curriculum offers engaging lessons that incorporate several modes of learning: visual, auditory, kinesthetic, verbal, logical, social, and solitary. For teachers, MathSEALs provides detailed lessons, as well as all the materials and resources you'll need to make teaching math a success. MathSEALs takes the toughest math standards and provides tech-flexible and engaging lesson plans to encourage student success.

One Drop of Kindness by Jeff Kubiak

Kindness...for some, it comes so easy, but for others, it can be a struggle. The answer often lies in a person's story. This book, along with each of you, will change our world as we know it. It only takes One Drop of Kindness to fill a heart with love.

The Fire Within by Mandy Froehlich

Adversity itself is not what defines us. It is how we react to that adversity and the choices we make that creates who we are and how we will persevere. The Fire Within: Lessons from defeat that have ignited a passion for learning is a compilation of stories from amazing educators who have faced personal adversity head on and have become stronger people for it!

Notes

Notes

Notes

Notes

EduMatch Publishing